Mum and

For Laura

First published individually as

Bend and Stretch (1987), *Dad's Back* (1985),

Making Friends (1987), *Messy Baby* (1985),

Mum's Home (1987), *Reading* (1985),

Sleeping (1985) and *This Little Nose* (1987)

by Walker Books Ltd

87 Vauxhall Walk, London SE11 5HJ

This edition published 1996

10 9 8 7 6 5 4 3 2 1

© 1985, 1987 Jan Ormerod

This book has been typeset in Bembo Educational.

Printed in Singapore

British Library Cataloguing in Publication Data

A catalogue record for this book is available from the British Library.

ISBN 0-7445-4448-3

Dad and Me

Jan Ormerod

Dad and Me

Mum and Me

WALKER BOOKS

AND SUBSIDIARIES

LONDON • BOSTON • SYDNEY

Dad and Me

Playing

Dad's back with jingling keys,
warm gloves, a cold nose ...

a long, long scarf
and apples in a bag.

11

Dad's back with a game,

a chase

and a tickle.

13

Reading

climbing over

crawling under

pushing through,
climbing up

relaxing

peeping over

reading

Sleeping

peeping

tickling

climbing up

bouncing

pulling his nose

cuddling

Messy Baby

Dad says,

"Soft toys in the box."

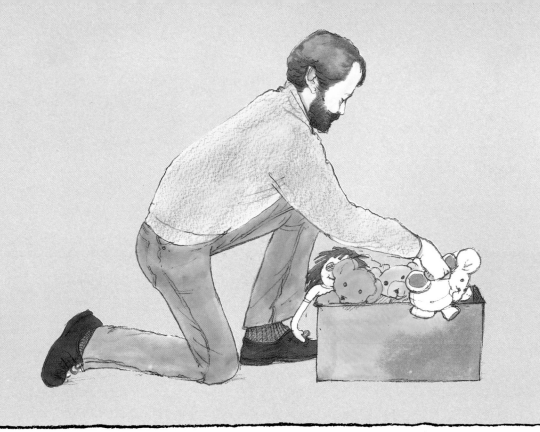

He says,

   "Books on the shelf."

Dad says, "Clothes in the cupboard.

He says, "Rubbish in the basket.

Bricks in the cart."

Food off the floor."

"Oh no, what a mess!
Oh, you messy baby!"

"Never mind," Dad says.
"Let's start again."

Mum and Me

Shopping

Mum's home.

What's in her basket?

Things for a baby.

Basket

And what else?

29

Dig deep.

Blow Mum's nose.

Have a banana …

31

and a snooze.

Making

Playing with
pieces of cloth.

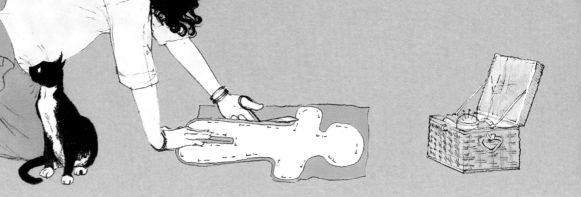

Resting on a pillow.

34

Friends

Playing with

reels of thread.

Playing with buttons.

Playing with wool.

Sitting together.

Making friends
with someone new.

Cuddling.

This Little

This little nose
    is red and runny.

This little nose
    is a very little nose.

This little nose
    is a long nose.

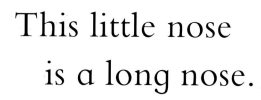

Nose

Who's a nosy,
furry fellow?

Two little noses
close together.

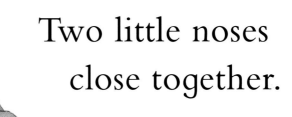

You'll feel better
in the morning.

Bend and

Breathe
   in and up.

Left leg, right leg,
   round and round.

Stretch

Breathe out
and down.

Stretching
that way.

Stretching
this way.

Tickle, tickle, tickle.
Giggle, giggle, giggle.

In, out, up, down,
round and round.

Rest and relax.